DRESSAGE TEST TECHNIQUE

by
Judy Harvey FBHS

Illustrations by
Carole Vincer

KENILWORTH PRESS

Copyright © 1994 The Kenilworth Press Ltd

First published in the UK in 1994
by Kenilworth Press, an imprint of Quiller Publishing Ltd

Reprinted 1994, 1996, 1999, 2002, 2005, 2008, 2011

British Library Cataloguing-in-Publication Data
A catalogue record for this book
is available from the British Library

ISBN 978 1 872082 51 6

Printed in China

Kenilworth Press

An imprint of Quiller Publishing Ltd
Wykey House, Wykey, Shrewsbury, SY4 1JA
Tel: 01939 261616 Fax: 01939 261606
E-mail: info@quillerbooks.com
Website: www.kenilworthpress.com

CONTENTS

Introduction

The fastest growing of the equestrian disciplines, dressage is the systematic, gymnastic development of the horse. The object is to improve the horse's natural paces and physique, making him more beautiful and impressive in his movement.

This guide is aimed at the rider who is just starting out in dressage competitions. Further information about riding and schooling can be found in earlier books in the series.

Dressage tests are designed as a progressive means of assessing the horse's development. At the lower levels (e.g. Preliminary and Novice in the UK) the tests are very basic in their demands and well within the capabilities of most horses and riders.

The requirements at Novice level are:

♦ Three correct basic paces – i.e. a walk with an even four-time beat; a trot that springs from one diagonal pair of legs to the other in a pronounced two-time rhythm; a canter that is clearly three-time with a moment of suspension, when all four legs are off the ground.

♦ A correct outline, with the horse accepting the bit.

♦ The horse should show correct bend in turns and circles and be straight when required.

♦ Transitions between one pace and another should be smooth and without resistance.

♦ The rider should have a well enough established seat to enable him to apply the aids correctly and to give the impression that he and the horse are working as a partnership.

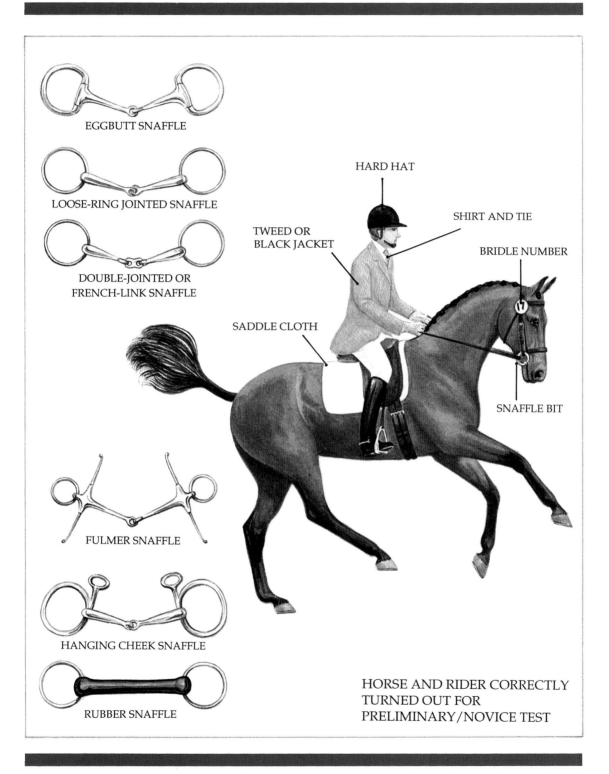

EGGBUTT SNAFFLE

LOOSE-RING JOINTED SNAFFLE

DOUBLE-JOINTED OR
FRENCH-LINK SNAFFLE

FULMER SNAFFLE

HANGING CHEEK SNAFFLE

RUBBER SNAFFLE

HARD HAT

SHIRT AND TIE

TWEED OR
BLACK JACKET

BRIDLE NUMBER

SADDLE CLOTH

SNAFFLE BIT

HORSE AND RIDER CORRECTLY
TURNED OUT FOR
PRELIMINARY/NOVICE TEST

Training, homework and preparation

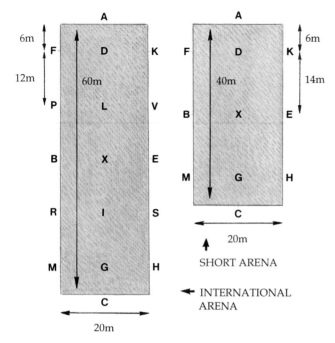

A

6m
F   D   K

12m
      60m

P   L   V

B   X   E

R   I   S

M   G   H

C

20m

A

6m
F   D   K

      40m   14m

B   X   E

M   G   H

C

20m

SHORT ARENA

← INTERNATIONAL ARENA

Training for a dressage test requires a disciplined approach. The horse requires regular schooling to develop and maintain his suppleness. How often will depend on your own limitations on time and facilities.

It is almost essential to have some help from a dressage trainer. A good trainer will help you to reach your potential. He will be happy to devise a training programme to fit in with your schedule. He will also be able to analyse your work from a judge's angle and point out ways in which to achieve better marks.

You will find it invaluable to school your horse in an area of the correct size. It does not have to be a proper arena – you can mark out an area in the field – but avoid schooling when the ground is hard or slippery.

One of the most useful training aids is a video camera. If you can get a friend to video your lessons you will have an invaluable insight into what you actually look like. How often have you been told to sit up when you thought you already were? It will reinforce what your trainer is trying to put across and help to remind you of his advice. It can be difficult to make notes when you are riding!

There are often professionals taking videos at competitions. Get your test videoed, sit down at home and analyse it together with the judge's sheet. It will help you to understand your marks. The video needs to be taken from as near as possible to the judge's position. It can be great fun to look back in future years and see how much you have progressed.

Learning the test

The choice of which test is most suited to your horse needs some consideration. Once you have got your show schedule, send off for copies of the tests being used and read through them carefully.

Preliminary and Novice tests are quite straightforward but some are more difficult than others. In Britain the tests are numbered in order of the degree of difficulty for the average horse and rider, so Novice Test 21 will be easier than Novice Test 28, for example. This is very much a general rule and does not take into account a horse's natural talent. For instance, your horse may find it easy to lengthen his stride in trot, but find the same movement in canter very difficult. To begin with, try to find a test that has movements well within your capabilities.

Reading through the test for the first time will give the impression that it is very easy and that it involves nothing that you and your horse couldn't do. The problems tend to arise when the movements are linked together and you are not allowed to make an extra circle in between. Riding transitions accurately at markers is very different to riding them when the moment feels right.

Once you have selected your test, learn it thoroughly. Do not rely on having someone call it for you. Commanders (callers) are not always permitted, so check up on the rules. Problems tend to occur when the commander either can't keep up or gets too far ahead. Sometimes the wind is so strong that your commander's instructions lose their clarity.

Your horse will need to be prepared for each movement well in advance and therefore you need to know what's coming next. The sequence of movements should be burnt indelibly in your mind. Tests where commanders are used are unlikely to be successful as the rider tends to concentrate on what is being said rather than how his horse is going. If commanders are allowed, and if you feel you will go to pieces, then by all means use one but be aware that it is your responsibility to know the test.

A useful exercise to help you to learn your test is to draw it out on paper using a diagram of the arena. Ask a friend to test you. Go through it on foot. You can even do this on the living-room carpet! Beware of riding through it too many times, though, as your horse will learn to anticipate the movements and may try to carry them out before you reach the appointed marker. Practise the movements in isolation from each other, only occasionally putting two or three together.

You will need to develop some form of mental rehearsal. Find a time and a place when you will not be disturbed. In your mind go through each and every movement and how you will need to ride it to achieve perfection. Picture your horse's evasions and how you will cope with them. Driving to the event, go over your test out loud; ask your passenger to test you. When the time comes to ride the test, your mental preparation will enable you to deal instinctively with every eventuality.

Paces and rhythm

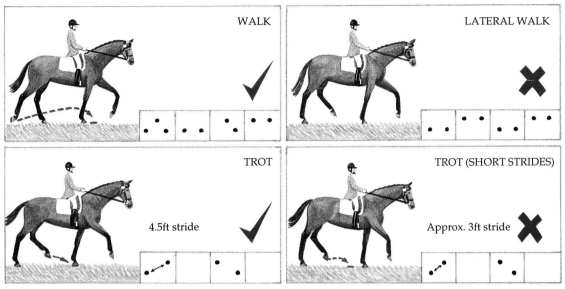

WALK

LATERAL WALK

TROT — 4.5ft stride

TROT (SHORT STRIDES) — Approx. 3ft stride

The object of dressage is to develop the horse's paces.

The walk: It is essential that the correct sequence is maintained - i.e. left hind, left fore, right hind, right fore, with four clear beats. In the early tests two types of walk are required. The *medium walk* requires the horse to be on the bit, making long but not extended strides. The *free walk* on a long rein is where the horse stretches his head and neck down, the rider allowing freedom but maintaining enough contact to prevent the reins swinging loose. The horse's stride should lengthen, and he should appear relaxed but keen and forwards.

Practise the transitions between free and medium walk. A common mistake is for the horse to jog when the reins are picked up, purely because he thinks he is going to be asked to trot.

The trot: Working trot and the ability to show a few lengthened strides, described later on, are required. In *working trot* the horse is on the bit, showing even steps, engaging the hindquarters. It is between *medium* and *collected* trot. Trot work easily shows up any tendency for the horse to be irregular, i.e. where he takes a shorter step with one leg. Usually a balance or stiffness problem, it can also mean that the horse is in physical pain. Irregular steps are heavily penalised and you should seek expert advice. Trot work should be ridden in a consistent rhythm, as if to a metronome.

The canter: *Working canter* shows the same qualities as working trot – active, light, and with engagement. A four-time canter shows a lack of engagement and is a serious fault.

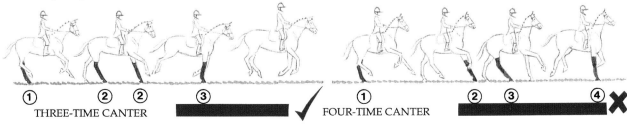

① ② ② ③
THREE-TIME CANTER

① ② ③ ④
FOUR-TIME CANTER

The centre line, halt and salute

Tests begin and end on the centre line, providing your judge with both first and last impressions of your performance.

Some of the more basic tests no longer require you to halt and salute at the beginning. With a young horse, the halt can disrupt the flow, causing resistance and loss of attention. However, these tests still begin by trotting down the centre line. Usually you will begin your test from outside the arena. Plan in advance which rein you intend to come in on. Your horse will be easier to keep straight if you make your turn off his stiffer rein, as he finds it less easy to curl up that way. Look for distractions, such as tubs of flowers. Is it possible to avoid them? The 'A' marker is also usually in the way.

Allow plenty of room to line up, off a smooth turn, with the centre line. Keep your horse straight by riding him forwards into his bridle. Line up the 'C' marker between his ears and look the judge straight in the eye. Practise the transition into halt; learn how much preparation your horse needs. The transition can be progressive at the lower levels, meaning that just one or two steps of walk can be shown between trot and halt. Once you have halted keep your horse still and straight. The judge at 'C'

cannot see his hind legs easily and is more likely to penalise crookedness and resistance to the bit.

To salute, put your reins and whip into one hand. If you are female or wearing a hat with a harness, drop your other arm straight down by your side and bow your head. Then raise your head and put your hand back on the reins. If you are male and not wearing a chin strap, remove your hat, lowering your arm to its full extent, then replace your hat and take back the reins. Practise saluting; your horse must learn to stand still and not be frightened by your hat.

Remember that your salute should be formal and dignified and is a mark of respect to your judge.

If your horse is very excited, refusing to stand still and perhaps even going backwards, then this is not the moment to give him a lesson in obedience. Carry out your salute and get going, or you could end up upsetting your horse even more. Make sure that you sort out the problem in training at home.

Your move-off must be straight, with an active transition from the halt. Position your horse in plenty of time for the turn at 'C', bend him correctly and have enough inside leg to keep a good rhythm.

Circles and turns

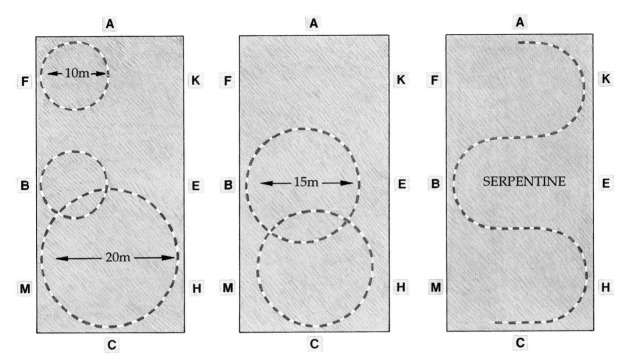

The secret of riding good circles and turns is preparation. When learning your test draw your circles to scale. See exactly where the tangents of the circle are in relation to the arena markers. When riding your horse be strict with yourself: make sure he is between leg and hand, staying on the line or curve that you want. Most novice horses try to make the circle smaller on their stiff rein, and find it easy to bulge out through the outside shoulder, making the circle bigger on the soft rein.

When riding a circle think of the word 'SOBER':

S - SHAPE of the circle.
O - OUTLINE, the horse on the bit.
B - BEND, correct for the movement.
E - ENERGY, with active engagement.
R - RHYTHM, regular even footfalls.

The same principles apply to all turns, loops and serpentines. They are really just parts of a circle. It is too easy just to let your horse shuffle round the corners. Every single turn needs to be prepared, putting the horse in the right balance with half-halts and then riding forward.

The serpentine asks for changes of bend and direction. It is a test of your horse's suppleness. To help perform a smooth change of rein, prepare the horse by bending him in the new direction, getting control of the new inside shoulder, before you actually allow him to turn and change direction. This must all be done without loss of balance and rhythm. Never allow him to 'prop' round, leaning on his inside shoulder.

Transitions

Transitions are changes from one pace to another or from one type of pace to another, e.g. from walk into trot or from working trot to medium trot. A perfect transition should be invisible. The first step of the new pace and the last step of the old pace should be as good in quality as the rest of the work. You do not want to see the horse shuffling to get his feet into the right place.

When riding a test, transitions are required at specific markers. This is when the rider's body is level with the marker. When the transitions are allowed to be progressive, the first step of the new pace should be at the marker. You will need to practise timing how much preparation your horse needs. The well-trained advanced horse will respond immediately to his rider's aids. Your horse might not

be quite so perfect and may need a little warning that something is coming!

Practise riding half-halts. Use them to prepare for a transition. Make them as discreet and invisible as possible – a secret code between you and your horse.

Always try to ride your transitions with as little use of the reins as possible. Of course you must keep a contact, but nothing is worse than the rider who pulls his horse into halt - the horse hollowing his back, throwing his head up and leaving his hind legs out behind him. Think of your horse's hind legs coming further under his body through a soft back and supple poll. Transitions are an excellent training exercise helping the horse to stay up off his forehand and developing his ability to lower his quarters and engage his hind legs.

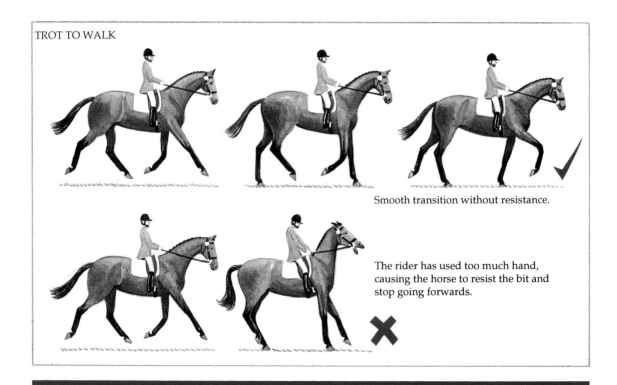

TROT TO WALK

Smooth transition without resistance.

The rider has used too much hand, causing the horse to resist the bit and stop going forwards.

Lengthening the stride

Lengthened strides in trot and canter are a requirement in many of the early tests.

The movement is a stepping stone towards showing medium and extended paces later on. Some horses have a natural talent for lengthening, others have to be taught.

The horse must be in the right balance with his hind legs well engaged. He must be straight, taking an even contact on both reins. The rhythm and the balance must be maintained.

To give the judge, at 'C', the best view, lengthened strides are usually ridden across the diagonal. This is not easy for the rider as he has not only to achieve the lengthening, but also to change the rein, keep the horse straight, and ride his corners.

The short side of the arena is used to get the horse engaged through half-halts and feeling really powerful. Turning onto the diagonal line, make sure that he is completely straight, then with both legs ask for more energy. Without allowing the horse to get on his forehand, allow just enough with your hands for him to lengthen his stride and outline. Keep the rhythm. Remember your downwards transition - ride the horse forwards and 'uphill' so that he comes back smoothly and without resistance.

In canter the same methods apply, except that you have to ride the downwards transition more carefully. There is a danger of the horse changing legs, becoming disunited or falling back to trot. You will need plenty of leg. Try to put the horse in a shoulder-in position, to keep him straight and the weight on his inside hind leg.

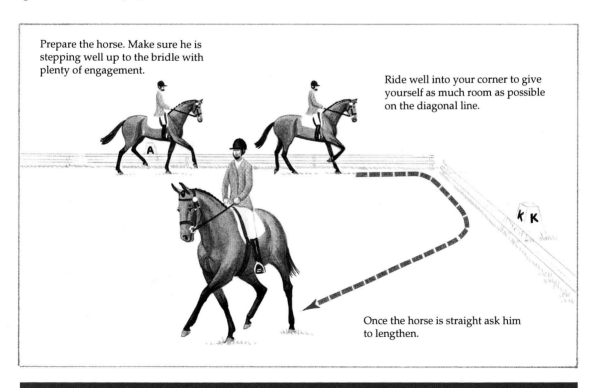

Prepare the horse. Make sure he is stepping well up to the bridle with plenty of engagement.

Ride well into your corner to give yourself as much room as possible on the diagonal line.

Once the horse is straight ask him to lengthen.

Give and retake the reins

This movement is designed to show that the horse is in 'self-carriage' and not balancing on the rider's hands. Ridden correctly, the rider pushes both hands forwards up the horse's neck so that the rein contact is completely loose for one or two strides. The horse's outline, balance and rhythm should remain the same. Common mistakes are that the horse rushes off, puts his head in the air, or falls back into trot.

Preparation is important in this movement. Half-halts will ensure self-carriage and that the horse accepts your legs, putting him in the right balance to be unaffected by the release of the rein. Some sensitive horses are disturbed when the rider moves his hands, so the movement does need practising to accustom the horse to it. It is an excellent training exercise.

The horse maintains his balance and outline as the contact is released.

Rein-back

This is a test of the horse's obedience. Correctly performed the horse steps back, picking his feet up in diagonal pairs. He should do this without tension or resistance and be so controlled that a precise number of steps can be achieved.

A good rein-back begins with a square halt, the rider's body level with the marker. The rider pushes the horse forward into a restraining hand, when the horse finds that he cannot go forward he then steps back. The main faults are: the horse refuses to step back at all; he is crooked or resistant; the steps might not be diagonal; or the horse rushes back dragging his feet. Practise the rein-back; learn which way your horse likes to push his quarters; feel how much leg he needs. Always move forwards again after the rein-back, and practise enough halts without reining back to make sure that the horse does not anticipate.

Counter-canter

Horse keeps same bend as in true canter.

Too much neck bend, losing balance and leaning on right shoulder.

Counter-canter is when the horse is cantering, for example on a circle to the left, with the right foreleg leading. He remains bent in the direction of the leading leg with the same amount of bend as in true canter. No more and no less. Counter-canter should look like a mirror-image of true canter. It is a suppling exercise and also a test of obedience. In the early tests, simple loops and half circles are all that are asked for.

Make it clear to the horse with your legs that you wish to stay in counter-canter. Your inside leg remains close to the girth, the outside leg further back, behind the girth. This is important for when you progress to flying changes later on. Always ride forwards, without rushing, and keep the horse balanced. Make sure that you keep the quarters under control and do not exaggerate the bend in the neck.

Do not repeat the exact movement required for the test too often, especially if it involves a transition back to trot as the horse will start to anticipate. He will come back to trot by himself, making it difficult to keep counter-canter all the way around the school.

Use counter-canter regularly in training; it will help your horse's development. It encourages the horse to put his hind legs more underneath him, and it is a tremendous help in straightening the canter.

Arriving at the show

- ◆ Allow plenty of time.
- ◆ Try to find a quiet place to park, preferably in the shade if it is hot.
- ◆ Declare your intention to compete to the secretary and find out which arena you are in. Check your number and your time.
- ◆ Check with your steward whether your class is running to time. Find out where you can ride-in.
- ◆ If possible watch some of your fellow competitors. See how the arena is riding – a slippery patch or a dip at 'X' may be avoided.
- ◆ Refresh your memory of the test; go through your mental rehearsal.
- ◆ Leave enough time for tacking-up and changing. It can take forever to tie a stock when you are nervous!
- ◆ If necessary, apply fly repellent and fit studs (if competing on grass).

Park your vehicle in a quiet, shady position if possible. Never leave your horse tied up outside your vehicle unattended.

Watch other competitors and learn from their mistakes. Note how the arena is riding.

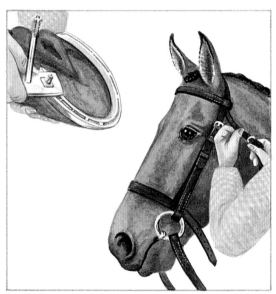

Studs are helpful when grass arenas are used. On artificial surfaces their disadvantages outweigh any advantage. Check your tack carefully.

Riding-in

Your objectives when riding-in are to produce the horse and yourself in the best physical and mental state to give your best performance. The time needed will depend on the individual horse. A sharp, lively type requires more work than a more placid horse which performs better when still fresh. Young horses are often difficult in this respect as they have a 'let's go crazy' period, followed by a short period of good work, followed by total exhaustion!

The weather also needs to be taken into consideration. Most horses require a longer period of riding-in on a cold, windy day; conversely, riders must be careful not to over-do things in hot, humid conditions. All horses require some riding-in to get their muscles warm and supple.

Remember to report to the steward and confirm your time, so you know how to plan you riding-in.

Riding-in areas are usually crowded. It is unfair and dangerous to take a fresh, naughty horse in amongst the other competitors. Make sure you observe the following rules:

♦ Pass left hand to left hand.

♦ Do not halt or walk on the track.

♦ Give way to those performing lateral work.

♦ If you need to adjust your tack, do so outside the area or well out of everybody's way.

♦ Do not be so intimidated that you forget to ride your horse well.

Practise some of the test movements, but if the going is unsuitable, don't overdo it.

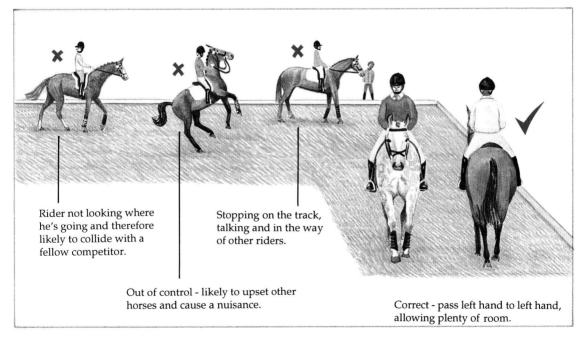

Rider not looking where he's going and therefore likely to collide with a fellow competitor.

Out of control - likely to upset other horses and cause a nuisance.

Stopping on the track, talking and in the way of other riders.

Correct - pass left hand to left hand, allowing plenty of room.

Final preparation

It is a great help to have someone on the ground to assist you. He can act as a mirror, telling you how the horse looks. Ten minutes before your turn, the brushing boots should be removed and you can put your jacket on. The girth should be checked and more fly repellent applied, if needed.

Arrive at the arena as soon as the horse before has finished. You will either have to ride around the outside of the arena or you may be allowed inside. Find out beforehand. The few moments before the test are vital to get the horse comfortable in the atmosphere. Some horses violently object to the judge's box, so make sure you ride past it. Don't forget to drop your whip if one is not permitted.

Judges don't like to be kept waiting. When you get the signal to start, return to the 'A' end of the arena and set up that perfect entry.

It is sensible to work your horse in with brushing boots on. Don't forget to remove them before your test.

Check your girth just before your test - the excitement of the show may have taken some weight off your horse.

Whips are sometimes not permitted. Check your rules. Make sure you drop your whip before you start your test.

Riding the test

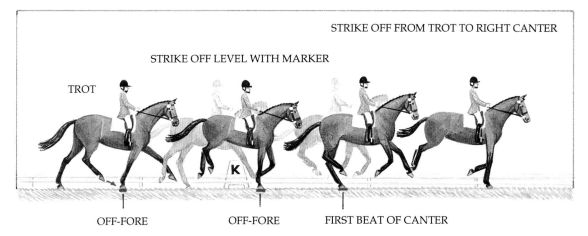

STRIKE OFF FROM TROT TO RIGHT CANTER

STRIKE OFF LEVEL WITH MARKER

TROT

OFF-FORE   OFF-FORE   FIRST BEAT OF CANTER

There is always a judge positioned at 'C'. Additional judges can be placed at 'E', 'B', 'H' and 'M'. This ensures that the test is judged from every angle. Be aware of where your judges are. For example, the judge at 'C' can tell if you are straight on the centre line but would find it difficult to see if your halt is exactly at 'X'. The judges at 'B' and 'E' have an excellent view of this but are less aware of any crookedness. This can explain the difference in the judges' marks. Use the 'A' end of the arena to correct the horse, preferably with the leg away from the judges.

Accuracy is important. Your circles must be round and your transitions at the markers. However, at the lower levels the judges prefer, within reason, to see smooth transitions without resistance rather than rough ones at the marker.

Try to ride a good rhythm into all your horse's paces and keep it through the movements.

If you need to use your voice make sure that none of the judges can hear.

A mistake may only affect one mark, so don't lose heart.

If you lose your way, don't panic; listen carefully to the judge's instructions about where to go next.

The movements will come up faster than you expect; you must think ahead and keep your horse balanced and on the aids.

Look pleased with your performance, smiling at the judge and rewarding your horse. You might convince them yet!

Judges on the side have a very different view from those at 'C'.

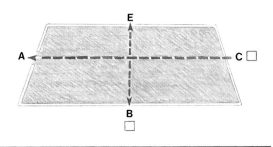

Analysing the judge's comments

LEANING ON FOREHAND

ABOVE THE BIT/OUTLINE NOT ROUND ENOUGH

Study your sheet – it will explain the judges' reasons for their marks. Below are some typical comments with some explanations.

Crooked - This will usually be qualified, e.g. quarters left, or weight on right shoulder.

Halt not square - This means that the horse has left a leg back in halt. It can be either a foreleg or a hind leg, usually the judge will say which. Timing and engagement in the transitions is the way to correct this.

Tilting head - This shows that the horse is not even in the rein contact and puts his nose to one side, indicating some stiffness.

Leaning on forehand – The horse gives the impression of pulling himself along, heavy in the rider's hands.

Short in neck – Does not refer to conformation but to the horse drawing back from the rider's hands, tightening the muscles in front of the withers. It also indicates that there is some stiffness and hollowing of the back.

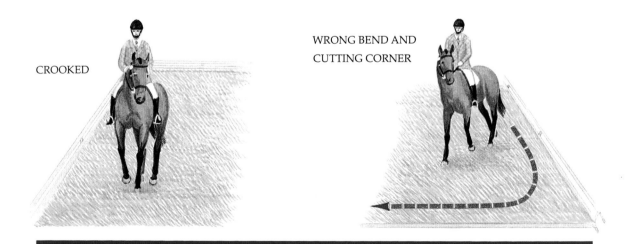

CROOKED

WRONG BEND AND CUTTING CORNER

TILTING

OVERBENT

SHORT IN NECK

Above the bit/Outline not round enough – This refers to the whole horse, not just the head and neck. The horse will be above the bit because he is not working from his hind legs through a supple back into the rein.

Overbent – The front of the horse's face is behind the vertical and he has dropped the bit. He is not genuinely taking the rein.

Falling in/Wrong bend/Cutting corner – Instead of keeping the correct bend around the rider's inside leg, the horse puts his weight on his inside shoulder going round the corner/circle like a motor bike, making it impossible to ride into the corners or ride correctly shaped figures.

Running – The horse loses his balance and cadence resulting in short, hurried steps.

Pacing/Irregular walk - This means that the horse is not walking in a correct four-time rhythm. It will be severely penalised.

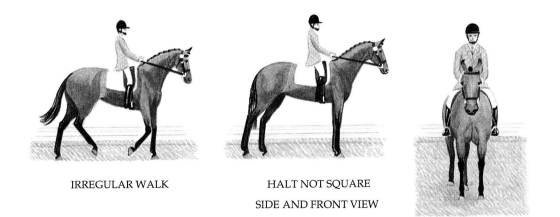

IRREGULAR WALK

HALT NOT SQUARE
SIDE AND FRONT VIEW

The collective marks

These convey the overall impression of the training of horse and rider. They are the most important marks and carry a coefficient of 2. A horse and rider who show natural talent and potential will get good collective marks. In the event of a 'tie' the total of the collective marks is sometimes used as the deciding factor.

PACES – *Freedom and regularity*
This mark rewards the correctness of all three paces. Sustained loss of regularity in any of the three paces during the test will lose marks, not only for that movement but for the paces as well. Brilliance and expression within the paces are rewarded here. A 16.2 hands horse that goes with short steps, like a pony, will not get a good mark for paces. Sometimes a horse will have a really good trot and canter, but a poor walk. The judge will not be able to give an 8 but will have to drop down to 6, which would be generous, or below. This mark reflects the judge's opinion of the horse's potential based on his performance in that test.

IMPULSION – *Desire to move forward, elasticity of the steps, suppleness of the back, and engagement of the hindquarters*
The horse will convey this through his willingness to go forward, pushing 'uphill' from his hind legs. Transitions within the pace are a good indicator of impulsion. Impulsion must be controlled and correctly channelled. Sometimes you see young horses showing off with excitement and misbehaving - this is not good impulsion. A horse which is pulling against the rider is not showing good impulsion either.

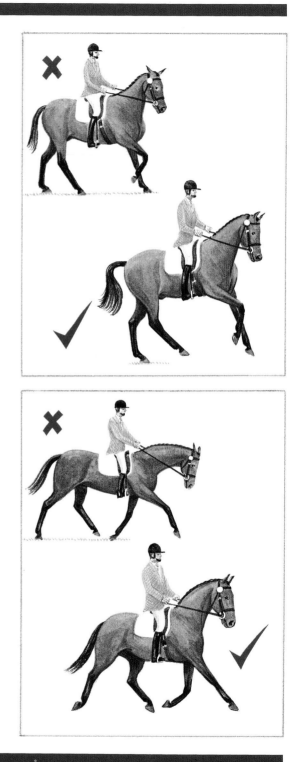

SUBMISSION – *Attention and confidence, harmony, lightness and ease of the movements, acceptance of the bridle and lightness of the forehand*
This mark reflects the correct training of the horse and also his willingness. Any resistance is marked down here. A true partnership, with horse and rider working well together, will be rewarded. Impulsion and submission are sometimes hard to separate as you can't have true lightness of the forehand without impulsion. The judge will give the lower mark to the category to which he wishes to draw the rider's attention.

THE RIDER – *Position, seat of rider and correct use of the aids*
The judge will consider that the rider is responsible for the horse's training and therefore its performance. The rider's mark will reflect what has gone on in the test.

The rider should appear elegant, sitting upright, with a supple seat, appearing at one with the horse. The aids should be applied discreetly and without roughness. A horse that has a problem with its mouth and resists the bit may be suggesting that its rider's hands are unacceptable. This will influence the rider's mark.

Sometimes you see a horse behaving so badly in a test that you think the rider deserves a medal for staying on. However, the judge has to consider that it is the rider's training which has caused this bad behaviour and will mark accordingly.

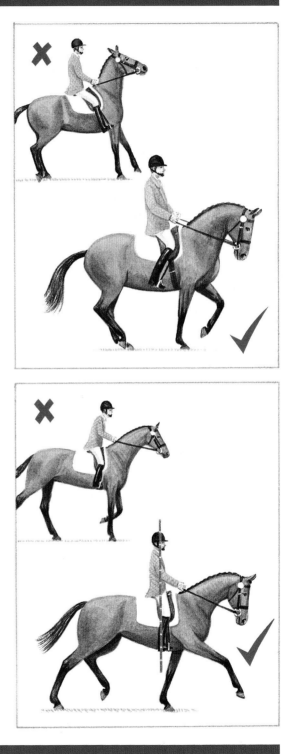

Ten points to remember

1. Have the best training that you can afford.

2. Choose a test well within your capabilities.

3. Learn the test thoroughly.

4. Practise the movements; make use of video.

5. Learn from watching others. Writing for a dressage judge will give you an insight into what the judges are looking for and what they can see.

6. Allow plenty of time on the day.

7. Think ahead when riding your test. Ride positively to show how good you are, not defensively to cover up mistakes.

8. Have your test videoed and compare it with your sheet. This will help you to understand the marks and comments.

9. If you are lucky enough to win, keep up the good work. Remember, it will be harder next time.

10. Finally, don't lose sight of the object of dressage: *'The harmonious development of the physique and ability of the horse, achieving perfect understanding with his rider.'*